The V

The Way of the Cross: this is the Spanish translation of the Latin expression *Via Crucis*. This Way, which follows the footsteps of Our Lord from Pilate's Praetorium to Mount Calvary, ends in the Tomb … We could also translate *Via Crucis* as the 'way of suffering' or the 'way of sorrows'.

Cross, sufferings, sorrows? What sense do these realities have in the context of our prayer? Aren't sufferings and sorrow the constant source of frustration to our human existence? Wouldn't it be more sensible – we can ask – to leave the memory of the passion and death of the Lord for other moments during the liturgical year? Isn't this just too sad …?

No: the *Via Crucis* is not an exercise in 'sadness'; nor does it belong to a caricature of Christianity that is full of sorrow, nor to a conception of the Christian life that is reduced to a set of obligations and lamentations flowing from a pessimistic vision of mankind and history. Cardinal Ratzinger – now Benedict XVI – gave an answer to this when he wrote of our need to overcome such deformed conceptions so as to enable us to accept the Christian proposal in its fullness; a proposal – he reminds us – that will not always be comfortable for human beings, but one that is certainly worthwhile: because only the truth makes us free, and only the truth brings complete joy.

The deep and liberating truth that we contemplate in the stations of the *Via Crucis* is this: that the second person of the Holy Trinity wanted, in a crazy act of love, to incarnate himself, to live and suffer freely for mankind: for each one of us – for you and for me – and to open the gates of eternal happiness for us. That is why, the surest translation of *Via Crucis*, which describes its essence most accurately, is the 'way of love'; and in a greater sense, the 'way of freedom and joy'.

Way of love

When we commemorate the sorrowful way of the cross of Our Lord, we call to mind and make present in a profound way, his redeeming love. A love that awaits a response in each one of us (- as popular wisdom reminds us, 'we repay love with love'); a love that enables us to overcome our natural fear of sacrifice and of self-renunciation – something which, in one way or another, we all experience.

Way of Calvary

Stations of the Cross
with
Pope Benedict XVI

All booklets are published thanks to the generous support of the members of the Catholic Truth Society

CATHOLIC TRUTH SOCIETY
PUBLISHERS TO THE HOLY SEE

Contents

On 24 April 2005, during the Mass inaugurating his pontificate, Benedict XVI reminded us of these words of his great predecessor in the Chair of Peter, Blessed John Paul II: "Do not be afraid!"

Such fears make us think that following the cross of Jesus is something that alienates and impoverishes us, when in fact, what happens is exactly the opposite: in the cross we find our love crucified, and when we embrace him with all our soul we find Love in capital letters, a love that gives us a joy that the world cannot give, and an intimate happiness that nothing and noone will be able to steal from us. 'Do not be afraid of Christ!" Benedict XVI said to the young people – "He takes nothing from you and gives you everything. Whoever gives to Him, receives a hundredfold. Yes, open wide the doors to Christ and you will find the true life!'.

Way of joy

We stand before one of the great Christian paradoxes: *The Way of the Cross* – the way of sorrow and of sacrifice – is at the same time a way of joy, because our faithful surrender to Christ brings us to meet true Love and this love produces joy. Therefore, praying the *Via Crucis* makes complete sense: contemplating the crucified love of Jesus Christ, fount of our joy.

At the foot of the cross, full of sorrow and love, we find Mary. This *Via Crucis* is illustrated by fourteen traditional Spanish '*pasos*' or moveable sculptures; they include one '*paso*' of the virgin Mary. It couldn't be any other way in the land of Spain, which John Paul II described as the land of Holy Mary. In this '*paso*', we contemplate our Mother, sorrowful, serene and strong, at the foot of the cross. Holy Mary gives us an unforgettable lesson in surrender, in free obedience, and love of God.

May this lesson stimulate in us an interior desire for conversion and a generous surrender to love, as God loves and in the ways that he wants of us. 'Have the courage to risk with a pure heart – Benedict XVI recommended. Commit yourself to God and then you will see that your life becomes greater and full of light because life is not boring, but full of infinite surprises as the infinite goodness of God is without end.

May God … bring many young people to experience the marvels of his love in their life, and enable them to respond to the great hope that God and the Church has placed in each one of them. May they discover in their journey through life this great word of hope – as the Pope reminded us – 'Only God, who embraced the universe, can propose and give to us that which, of ourselves we could never attain'.

May our meditation of the Lord's Passion increase our commitment to work for the kingdom of God. 'His kingdom' – the Pope reminded us – 'is not something distant or imaginary, part of a future that will never arrive. His kingdom is present today, wherever he is loved and where his love reaches us'.

And so we pray to Our Lady, at the foot of the cross. In Madrid she is called Our Lady of Almudena, a title linked to the Arabic term '*almudin*', or wheat market. She is Our Lady of unconditional self-giving; Our Lady of the wheat grain that flourished because it knew how to die to itself out of love; she is Our Lady of the harvest, the divine harvest for which the Lord awaits.

What a responsibility to know that he counts on us – on me and on you – to collect the harvest!

Be united to Christ

As on Good Friday afternoon, we will now accompany Jesus, the Son of God, in the mysteries of his dramatic and glorious Passion: mysteries of life and salvation, mysteries that reveal the love of Christ who 'loved us to the end', even to the point of giving his life for us. To meditate on the mysteries of Christ is an act of intense prayer which allows us to be united to Christ and to share in his sufferings, opening us up to his love and uniting our cross to his. Love makes itself present in compassion. Thus, as we contemplate Christ's passion, we make present the suffering of so many of our brothers and sisters who, through their own sins and the sins of others, wander through a vast *Via Crucis*, in danger of losing their faith and hope. Today we want to imitate Simon of Cyrene: so that by embracing Christ's cross we may in prayer and charity embrace the sorrows of others..

Invitation

In this time of prayer, we will accompany Christ in his journey to Mount Calvary to be crucified.

Let us reawaken our love, following close behind him. Let us keep a profound silence in the external environment and inside our minds, so as not to let thoughts that are foreign to this pious contemplation interrupt us.

Let us situate ourselves: with humility and asking for his grace, recognizing that we are not worthy of entering "into his heart" in order to think like He does, feel like He does and live like He does the mystery of pain that he assumed in his own flesh, to pay for the sins of humanity.

We will remember all the young people in the world who are victims of injustice, persecution, marginalization, harsh treatment, poverty, slaveries, vexations… to them Jesus says that they are not alone, because he takes on their pain and walks at their side.

'Come to me all you who labor and are burdened, and I will give you rest' (*Mt* 11:30).

First Station

The Last Supper with the Disciples

V. We adore you, O Christ, and we praise you.
R. Because by your holy cross you have redeemed
   the world.

Then he took the bread, said the blessing,
broke it, and gave it to them, saying, 'This is
my body, which will be given for you; do this
in memory of me.'

And likewise the cup after they had eaten,
saying, 'This cup is the new covenant in my
blood, which will be shed for you.
(Lk 22:19-20)

Meditation

Before taking the bread in his hands, Jesus welcomes with love all those who are seated at his table. He doesn't exclude anyone: not even the traitor, or the one who will deny him, nor those who will flee. He has chosen them as a new people of God. They are the Church and are called to be one body.

Jesus dies to unite the dispersed children of God (*Jn* 11:52). 'I pray not only for them, but also for those who will believe in me through their word, so that they may all be one' (*Jn* 17:20-21).

Love strengthens unity. And he says: Love one another (*Jn* 13:34). Faithful love is humble: you ought to wash one another's feet (*Jn* 13:14).

United in the prayer of Christ, we pray that in the Holy Land the Church may live united and in peace, that all persecution and discrimination because of faith may cease, and all who believe in one God may live in justice and fraternity until God grants us the grace to sit together at his table.

Our Father – Hail Mary – Glory be

Second Station

Judas betrays Christ with a kiss

V. We adore you, O Christ, and we praise you.
R. Because by your holy cross you have redeemed
    the world.

So he dipped the morsel and handed it to Judas, son of Simon the Iscariot. After he took the morsel, Satan entered him.
(*Jn* 13:26)

Immediately he went over to Jesus… and he kissed him. Jesus answered him, 'Friend, do what you have come for'. (Mt 26:49-50)

Meditation

The breeze of a sacred mystery can be felt in the Last Supper. Christ is serene, pensive, suffering. He had said: 'I have eagerly desired to eat this Passover with you before I suffer' (*Lk* 22:15).

And now, quietly, he lets his deepest sentiment escape: 'Amen, amen, I say to you, one of you will betray me' (*Jn* 13:21).

Judas feels bad; his ambition has traded "for the price of betrayal" the God of Love for the idol of money. Jesus looks at him and he turns aside. Jesus calls his attention offering him bread with sauce. And he says: 'What you are going to do, do quickly' (*Jn* 13:27).

Judas's heart has been hardened and he goes to count his money before handing Jesus over with a kiss. And Christ, feeling the coldness of the traitor's kiss, doesn't reproach him but says: 'friend.'

If you are feeling in your flesh the coldness of betrayal, or the terrible suffering provoked by division between brothers and sisters, turn to Jesus. Being kissed by Judas he made all painful betrayals his own.

Our Father – Hail Mary – Glory be

Third Station

Jesus is sentenced to death

V. We adore you, O Christ, and we praise you.
R. Because by your holy cross you have redeemed
    the world.

---

*He deserves to die! Then they spat in his face
and hit him with their fists; others said as
they struck him: 'Play the prophet, Christ!
Who hit you then?' (Mt 26:66-68)*

*Then he handed him over to be crucified and
carrying his own cross Jesus went out of the
city to the place of the skull... where they
crucified him. (Jn 19:16 ff)*

Meditation

The greatest injustice is to condemn an innocent and defenceless person and one day evil judged innocence and condemned it to death. Why did they condemn Jesus? Because Jesus took upon himself the pain of the world. When he became flesh he assumed our humanity, and with it the wounds of sin. Their guilt he shall bear (*Is* 53:11), in order to cure us through the sacrifice of the cross.

A man of suffering, accustomed to infirmity (*Is* 53:3), he surrendered himself to death (*Is* 53:12). What is most remarkable is Jesus' silence. He doesn't exonerate himself, he is the lamb of God who takes away the sin of the world (*Jn* 1:29) as he was whipped, crushed, and sacrificed. But he was silent and opened not his mouth (*Is* 53:7).

In God's silence all innocent victims of wars are present, wars that demolish peoples and sow hatred that is difficult to cure. Jesus remains silent in the heart of many people who quietly wait for God's salvation.

Our Father – Hail Mary – Glory be

Fourth Station

Peter's denial

V. We adore you, O Christ, and we praise you.
R. Because by your holy cross you have redeemed
   the world.

---

*'Will you lay down your life for me? Amen,
amen, I say to you, the cock will not crow
before you deny me three times'. (Jn 13:38)*

*He went out and began to weep bitterly.
Meanwhile the men who guarded Jesus
were mocking and beating him.
(Lk 22:62-63).*

Meditation

A Christian has to be brave and to be brave doesn't mean not to know fear, but to know how to conquer fear. A brave Christian doesn't hide in shame from manifesting his or her faith in public. Jesus warned Peter: 'Simon, Simon, behold Satan has demanded to sift all of you like wheat, but I have prayed that your own faith may not fail (*Lk* 22:31). I tell you, Peter, before the cock crows this day, you will deny three times that you know me' (*Lk* 22:34). And the apostle, for fear of some servants, denied him saying: 'I do not know him' (*Lk* 22:57). As Jesus was passing through one of the courtyards, he saw him… Peter trembles remembering his words… and cries with bitterness over his treachery. The gaze of God changes the heart. But we have to let ourselves be looked upon.

Looking at Peter, the Lord has turned his eyes toward those Christians who are ashamed of their faith, who lack courage to defend life from its natural beginning until its natural end, or those who want to be admired according to criteria that isn't the gospel… so that like Peter they recover their courage and become convinced witnesses of what they believe.

Our Father – Hail Mary – Glory be

Fifth Station

Jesus carries his cross

V. We adore you, O Christ, and we praise you.
R. Because by your holy cross you have redeemed
the world.

---

*And when they had mocked him, they
stripped him of the purple cloak, dressed
him in his own clothes, and led him out to
crucify him. (Mk 15:20)*

*And carrying the cross himself he went out
to what is called the Place of the Skull, in
Hebrew, Golgotha. (Jn 19:17)*

Meditation

The cross is not merely a piece of wood. The cross represents everything that makes life difficult. Among crosses, the deepest and most painful is the one that is rooted inside of a person. It is the sin that hardens the heart and perverts human relationships. For from the heart come evil thoughts, murder, adultery, unchastity, theft, false witness, blasphemy (*Mt* 15:19). The cross that Jesus carried on his shoulders to later die upon is the weight of all the sins of mankind, my sins as well. He himself bore our sins in his body upon the cross (1 *P* 2:24). Jesus dies to reconcile all men with God and this makes the cross 'redemptive.' But the cross by itself doesn't save us. It is the crucified one who saves us.

He made his own; the tiredness, exhaustion, and endurance of those who don't find work, of the immigrants who receive unworthy or inhumane offers of work, who suffer from racist attitudes or die in the effort to obtain a more just and human life.

Our Father – Hail Mary – Glory be

Sixth Station

Jesus falls beneath the weight of the cross

V. We adore you, O Christ, and we praise you.
R. Because by your holy cross you have redeemed
the world.

---

*He was pierced through our faults. He was
crushed for our sins... through his wounds
we are healed.* (Is 53:5)

*Jesus fell beneath the weight of the cross
various times on the path to Calvary.*
(Translation of the Church in Jerusalem).

Meditation

Sacred Scripture doesn't make any reference to Jesus falling, but it is logical that he would lose his balance many times. The loss of blood because of the scourging which tore the skin, the unbearable muscular pain, the torture of the crown of thorns, the weight of the wood… words are not enough. We have all experienced stumbling and falling to the ground. How quickly we get back up so as not to make a show! Contemplate Jesus on the ground and all those around him; see him receive one blow and then another so that he could not get up on his own. How they ridicule him! What a humiliation. The psalm says, 'But I am a worm, hardly human, scorned by everyone, despised by the people. All who see me mock me; they curl their lips and jeer; they shake their heads at me (*Ps* 22:7-8).

Jesus suffers with all those who trip on stones and fall victims to alcohol, drugs and other dependencies that make them slaves, so that supporting themselves in him, and in those who come to their aid, they may get up again.

Our Father – Hail Mary – Glory be

Seventh Station

*Simon of Cyrene helps Jesus
to carry his cross*

V. We adore you, O Christ, and we praise you.
R. Because by your holy cross you have redeemed
the world.

———————————

*As they led him away they took hold of a
certain Simon, a Cyrenian, who was coming
in from the country. (Lk 23:26)*

*This man they pressed into service to carry
his cross. (Mt 27:32)*

———————————

Meditation

Simon was a strong young farmer who was coming from his work in the fields. They forced him to carry the cross of Our Lord, moved not by compassion but out of fear that Jesus would die on the way. Simon resisted, but the soldiers insisted. He had to accept under coercion. Through contact with Jesus, the attitude of his heart started to change and he ended up sharing the situation of that stranger who was being executed, who in silence carried a weight heavier than his weak strength could bear. How important it is that we Christians discover what is happening beside us and realize that there are people who need us.

Jesus felt respite through the help of the Cyrenian. Thousands of young people of all races, conditions and creeds, marginalized by society, daily encounter Cyrenians who know how to embrace the cross and walk beside them with generous self-giving.

Our Father – Hail Mary – Glory be

Eighth Station

Veronica wipes the face of Jesus

V. We adore you, O Christ, and we praise you.
R. Because by your holy cross you have redeemed
the world.

---

*A large crowd of people followed Jesus,
including many women who mourned and
lamented him. Jesus turned to them and
said, "Daughters of Jerusalem, do not weep
for me; weep instead for yourselves and for
your children". (Lk 23:27-28)*

*The LORD keeps and preserves them, makes
them happy in the land, and does not betray
them to their enemies. (Ps 41:3)*

Meditation

A large crowd of people followed Jesus, including many women who mourned and lamented him. Jesus turned to them and said, 'Do not weep for me; weep instead for yourselves and for your children'. Cry, not with sad weeping that hardens the heart and predisposes one to produce new crimes… cry, with soft weeping that cries out to heaven, begging for mercy and forgiveness. One of the women, moved on seeing the Lord's face covered in blood, dirt and spit, made her way valiantly past the soldiers until she arrived at Jesus. She took off her headscarf and wiped his face gently. A soldier drew her back violently, yet, looking at the headscarf, she saw that Christ's bloodied and suffering face was traced upon it.

Jesus is moved to compassion on seeing the women of Jerusalem and in Veronica's cloth leaves an image of his face. This calls to mind the faces of those who have been disfigured by atheist regimes that destroy the person and take away their human dignity.

Our Father – Hail Mary – Glory be

Ninth Station

Jesus is stripped of his garments

V. We adore you, O Christ, and we praise you.
R. Because by your holy cross you have redeemed
the world.

———————

*Then they crucified him and divided his
garments by casting lots for them to see
what each should take. (Mk 15:24)*

*From the sole of the foot to the head there
is no sound spot. Without beauty, without
majesty we saw him, no looks to attract our
eyes; despised and rejected by man. (Is 1:6)*

———————

Meditation

While the executioners prepared the nails and the ropes to crucify him, Jesus remained standing. A merciless soldier came close, and pulled on his tunic, ripping it off. The wounds began to bleed again causing a terrible pain. Then they divided his garments among them. Jesus was left naked in front of the masses. Like an object of cruel jokes they stripped him of everything. There is no greater humiliation, no greater scorn. They have left him entirely disarmed. Garments don't only cover the body but also maintain human dignity. Jesus went through this shame because he bears the weight of all sins against integrity and purity and died to take away the sins of all (*Heb* 9:28).

Jesus suffers with all those who are victims of human genocide where brutal violence explodes. He suffers with victims of rape and sexual abuse, and all those who are stripped of their dignity, of their innocence, of their trust in man.

Our Father – Hail Mary – Glory be

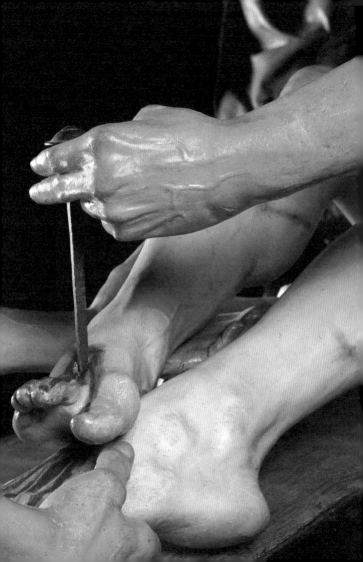

Tenth Station

Jesus is nailed to the cross

V. We adore you, O Christ, and we praise you.
R. Because by your holy cross you have redeemed
the world.

---

*When they came to the place called the
Skull, they crucified him and the criminals
there, one on his right, the other on his left.
(Lk 23:33)*

*Harshly dealt with, he bore it humbly... like
a lamb led to the slaughter. (Is 53:7)*

Meditation

They had led Jesus to Golgotha. He didn't go alone, but was accompanied by two thieves who would also be crucified. There they crucified him, and with him two others, one on either side, with Jesus in the middle (*Jn* 19:18). What a graphic image! The lamb who takes away the sin of the world, becomes sin and pays for the rest. The great sin of the world is "the lie of Satan". And they condemn Jesus for declaring the truth that he is the Son of God. The truth, that is the argument that justifies the crucifixion. It is impossible to describe what Christ suffered physically in his body as he hung on the cross; what he suffered morally, on being hung naked in between evildoers; and emotionally on finding himself abandoned by those who were his own.

Jesus on the cross embraces the suffering of all those who live nailed to painful situations, such as parents and young people who because of lack of work, live precariously, in poverty or desperation, without the resources necessary to make their families pull through and live a dignified life.

Our Father – Hail Mary – Glory be

Eleventh Station

Jesus dies on the cross

V. We adore you, O Christ, and we praise you.
R. Because by your holy cross you have redeemed
   the world.

---

*Jesus cried out in a loud voice, 'Father, into
your hands I commend my spirit'; and when
he had said this he breathed his last.*
(*Lk* 23:46)

*But when they came to Jesus and saw that
he was already dead, they did not break his
legs.* (*Jn* 19:33)

Meditation

It was the Sabbath, the day of preparation for the feast of the Passover. Pilate authorized them to break the criminals' legs in order to hurry their death so that they might not stay hanging on the crosses during the feast.

Jesus had already died and a soldier, in order to make sure, thrust a lance into his side. For this happened so that the scripture passage might be fulfilled: 'Not a bone of it will be broken.' And again another passage says: 'They will look upon him whom they have pierced' (*Jn* 19:36-37).

The sun was darkened and the veil of the Temple was torn in two. The earth shook… this is a sacred moment of contemplation. This is the moment of adoration… when we situate ourselves in front of the body of our Redeemer: lifeless, crushed, tortured, hanging… paying the price for our evils, "for my evils"…

I have sinned, Lord, have mercy on me, a sinner!
Amen.

Jesus dies for me. Jesus gains the Father's mercy
for me. Jesus pays for all that I should have
paid for. And what will I do for him? Before the
drama of so many crucified people with different
handicaps, do I fight to extend and proclaim the
dignity of the person and the Gospel of life?

Our Father – Hail Mary – Glory be

Twelfth Station

Jesus is taken down from the cross

V. We adore you, O Christ, and we praise you.
R. Because by your holy cross you have redeemed
the world.

---

*Pilate ordered the body of Jesus to be
handed over.* (*Mt* 27:57)

*Taking the body, Joseph wrapped it in clean
linen.* (*Mt* 27:59)

*His soul's anguish over, he shall see the
light and be content.* (*Is* 53:11)

Meditation

Let us come close to the Virgin Mary and share her sorrow. Christ has died and has to be taken down from the cross. What must be going through her mind? Who will help me take him down? Where will I put his body? And she must have repeated what she had said in Nazareth: 'Let it be done!' But now she is more united to the unconditional self-giving of her Son: 'It is finished'. Then Joseph of Arimathea and Nicodemus appeared, who, though they belonged to the Sanhedrin, hadn't taken part in the death of the Lord and had asked Pilate for the body of the Teacher in order to bury it in a new tomb that was theirs, which was very close to Calvary.

Christ had failed, making his own the failures of all humanity. The Son of Man had been eliminated, sharing the lot of those who for different reasons have been considered the dross of humanity, because they don't know better, or aren't capable, or seem to be unworthy. They are, among others, the victims of AIDS who, suffering their own wounds of the cross, hope that someone will take care of them.

Our Father – Hail Mary – Glory be

Thirteenth Station

Jesus is held in Mary's arms

V. We adore you, O Christ, and we praise you.
R. Because by your holy cross you have redeemed
the world.

And you yourself a sword will pierce.
(Lk 2:34)

Look and see if there is sorrow like my
sorrow. (Lm 3:20)

His mother stored all these things in her
heart. (Lk 2:51)

Meditation

Although we are all guilty of the death of Jesus, in these sorrowful moments the Virgin Mary needs our love and closeness. Our awareness of being repentant sinners will console her. With filial love let us place ourselves at her side, and let us learn to receive Jesus with the tenderness and love with which she received the mangled, lifeless body of her Son in her arms. Is there sorrow like my sorrow? And as they prepare the body of the Lord for burial 'according to the Jewish burial custom', Mary, adoring the Mystery that she had kept in her heart without having understood it, deeply moved, repeats with the prophet, 'O my people, what have I done to you, or how have I wearied you? Answer me!' (*Mi* 6:3).

As we contemplate the sorrow of the Virgin Mary, we recall the sorrow and loneliness of so many parents who have lost their children through starvation, while opulent societies, eaten up by consumerism and by the perversion of materialism, are sunk in the nihilism of empty lives.

Our Father – Hail Mary – Glory be

Fourteenth Station

Jesus is placed in the tomb

V. We adore you, O Christ, and we praise you.
R. Because by your holy cross you have redeemed
the world.

---

*So they laid Jesus there because of the
Jewish preparation day; for the tomb was
close by. (Jn 19:42)*

*Joseph of Arimathea ... rolled a huge
stone across the entrance to the tomb and
departed. (Mt 27:60)*

Meditation

Because the feast was close at hand, they hurriedly prepared the body of the Lord to be placed in the tomb that Joseph and Nicodemus offered. The tomb was new; no one had been buried there. Once the body had been placed there, Joseph had a stone rolled in the place of a door, and the entrance was closed. Unless a grain of wheat should fall to the ground and die… and once the noise of the rock closing off access to the tomb had ceased, Mary, in the silence of a striking loneliness, tightens her grip on the grain of wheat that she carries in her heart, like the first fruit of the Resurrection.

With this grain of wheat we remember the humble work and sacrifice of so many lives spent in selfless service of God and neighbour, who wait united to the death of Jesus. We remember all Good Samaritans, who appear in every corner of the earth and share the consequences of the terrible powers of nature: earthquakes, hurricanes, and tsunamis.

Our Father – Hail Mary – Glory be

The wisdom of the Cross

We have celebrated this *Way of the Cross* with fervour and devotion, following Christ along the path of his passion and death. The commentaries of the *Little Sisters of the Cross*, who serve the poor and most needy, have helped us enter into the mystery of Christ's glorious cross, wherein is found God's true wisdom which judges the world and judges those who consider themselves wise (cf. 1 *Cor* 1:17-19). We have also been assisted on this journey to Calvary by our contemplation of these wonderful images from the religious patrimony of the Spanish dioceses. In these images, faith and art combine so as to penetrate our heart and summon us to conversion. When faith's gaze is pure and authentic, beauty places itself at its service and is able to depict the mysteries of our salvation in such a way as to move us profoundly and transform our hearts, as Saint Teresa of Jesus herself experienced while contemplating an image of the wounded Christ (cf. *Autobiography*, 9:1).

As we were making our way with Jesus towards the place of his sacrifice on Mount Calvary, the words of Saint Paul came to mind: 'Christ loved me and gave himself for me' (*Ga* 2:20). In the face of such disinterested love, we find ourselves asking, filled with wonder and gratitude: What can we do for him? What response shall we give him? Saint John puts it succinctly: 'By this we know love: that he laid down his life for us; and we ought to lay down our lives for the brethren' (1 *Jn* 3:16). Christ's passion urges us to take upon our own shoulders the sufferings of the world, in the certainty that God is not distant or far removed from man and his troubles. On the contrary, he became one of us 'in order to suffer with man in an utterly real way — in flesh and blood ... hence in all human suffering we are joined by one who experiences and carries that suffering with us; hence con-solatio is present in all suffering, the consolation of God's compassionate love — and so the star of hope rises' (*Spe Salvi*, 39).

The mysterious wisdom of the cross

May Christ's love for us increase your joy and encourage you to go in search of those less fortunate. You are open to the idea of sharing your lives with others, so be sure not to pass by on the other side in the face of human suffering, for it is here that God expects you to give of your very best: your capacity for love and compassion. The different forms of suffering that have unfolded before our eyes in the course of this *Way of the Cross* are the Lord's way of summoning us to spend our lives following in his footsteps and becoming signs of his consolation and salvation. 'To suffer with the other and for others; to suffer for the sake of truth and justice; to suffer out of love and in order to become a person who truly loves — these are fundamental elements of humanity, and to abandon them would destroy man himself' (*Spe Salvi*, 39).

Let us eagerly welcome these teachings and put them into practice. Let us look upon Christ, hanging on the harsh wood of the cross, and let us ask him to teach us this mysterious wisdom of the cross, by which man lives. The cross was not a sign of failure, but an expression of self-giving in love that extends even to the supreme sacrifice of one's life. The Father wanted to show his love for us through the embrace of his crucified Son: crucified out of love. The cross, by its shape and its meaning, represents this love of both the Father and the Son for men. Here we recognize the icon of supreme love, which teaches us to love what God loves and in the way that he loves: this is the Good News that gives hope to the world.

Let us turn our gaze now to the Virgin Mary, who was given to us on calvary to be our Mother, and let us ask her to sustain us with her loving protection along the path of life, particularly when we pass through the night of suffering, so that we may be able to remain steadfast, as she did, at the foot of the cross.

Final prayer

Our Lady and Our Mother,
you remained firm in the faith,
united to the passion of your Son.
As we come to the end of this *Via Crucis*,
we turn our eyes and our hearts to you.

Unworthy as we are,
we welcome you into our house.
We welcome you as our Mother.
as did the Apostle, John.

We are with you Mary in your solitude
and offer you our companionship,
as you sustain the sorrow of so many of our
brothers and sisters,
who complete in their flesh
that which is lacking in the passion of Christ,
for his body,
which is the Church.

Look upon them with a Mother's love,
wipe away their tears,
heal their wounds, and increase their hope,
so that they may ever experience the cross
as the way to glory,
and the passion as the prelude to resurrection.

Amen.

Sources

This text is drawn largely from the *Way of the Cross* celebrated by Pope Benedict XVI in the Plaza Colon-Plaza Cibeles, Madrid, on 19 August 2011, during his apostolic journey to Madrid on the occasion of the 26th World Youth Day.

The *Way of the Cross*: from an introductory address made at the celebration by Antonio Maria Rouco Varela, Cardinal Archbishop of Madrid.

Be United to Christ: from the opening remarks made by His Holiness Pope Benedict XVI at the celebration; from an admonitary invitation made as the celebration began.

The Stations: The reflections on the Stations of the Cross were composed by the Sisters of the Cross (Hermanas de la Cruz) who take care of the poorest of the poor.

The Wisdom of the Cross: text of the address made by His Holiness Pope Benedict XVI after the meditation on the fourteen stations.

Final Prayer: made by His Holiness Pope Benedict XVI at the conclusion of the celebration.

Images of the Staions

Images of the fourteen traditional Spanish 'pasos', reproduced with thanks, were assembled in Madrid for this *Via Crucis*, thanks to the generous effort of many Brotherhoods and Confraternities from all the regions of Spain. Details of the artists are availbale from the publisher.